# U

*is for*

# Undoing

# Magick

## Kitchen Table Magick Series

*by*
### G. Alan Joel

# Esoteric School of Shamanism & Magic

Email: *alan@shamanschool.com*
Website: *www.shamanschool.com*

Publisher: Esoteric School of Shamanism and Magic, Inc.

Disclaimer and Legal Notice:
The Esoteric School of Shamanism and Magic has made every effort to ensure, at the time of this writing, that the information contained in this book is as accurate as possible. The publisher and author make no warranties or representation with respect to the completeness, fitness, accuracy, applicability, or appropriateness of this book's contents. This book's information is provided strictly for entertainment and educational purposes. Should you choose to use or apply the ideas provided in this book, you take full responsibility for your own actions. The publisher and author provide no guarantee that your life will improve in any way should you choose to use the information presented in this book. The ability of the information provided in this book to provide self-help and life improvement to the reader is entirely dependent upon the reader. The reader's ability to gain positive results from the information presented in this book is entirely dependent on the amount of time the reader devotes to the application of the material in this book, the willingness of the reader to dedicate time and effort to learning the materials presented in this book, as well as the reader's own belief system, which may help or hinder the reader's ability to benefit from this book's materials. Since each reader differs according to willingness and openness to the information available in this book, the author and publisher cannot guarantee success or improvement for every individual reader. Neither the publisher nor the author assumes responsibility for the reader's actions, or whether the information is used for negative or positive purposes. The information contained in this book is drawn from tribal traditions—both modern and ancient—as well as the author's 30 plus years' experience researching and teaching this material to students. The information in this book is presented as interpreted by the author, and, as such, may or may not be entirely accurate. In no way should the information presented in this book be a substitute for advice from health or mental health professionals. The author and publisher are not liable—or in any way responsible—for actions

[this page intentionally left blank]

# *Undoing Magick Blessing*

Child of Wonder,
Child of Flame
Nourish Our Spirits and
Protect Our Aim.

We all make mistakes, this be true,
Or have oopsie events that can make us blue.
When the outcomes are not what we seek,
Undoing magick is the way to a future less bleak!

The Four Elements of Air, Fire, Water, and Earth,
Can be the key to undoing magick of great worth.
A simple pendulum be a powerful undoing magick tool,
For it unwinds the most dastardly results of being a fool!

If someone bothers you with spells and unwanted energy,
Undoing magick helps you send it back with twice the
urgency.
Basic objects like a certain stone or a cup of coffee,
Be tools of undoing magick that can be carried out with great
glee!

Undoing magick is practical, fun, and effective, too.

It's simple magick that releases you from most catch-22s.
With practice you soon realize that undoing magick is very
cool,
And the tools of undoing magick are all around you!

Thus my will, so mote it be!

[this page intentionally left blank]

# Free Gift

To thank you for purchasing this book, I'd like to give you a

100% FREE GIFT

Learn more about your free magickal gift.

## Access Your Free Gift at www.shamanschool.com

**Find a complete list of magickal resources on https://amzn.to/3swxvPo. These resources are constantly updated so check back often!**

# Kitchen Table Undoing Magick
## Table of Contents

[this page intentionally left blank]

# Introduction to Kitchen Table Undoing Magick

*"We're asking you to trust in the Well-being. In optimism there is magic."*
*~ Abraham*

## A Note About This Introduction

This book is one of a series of books in the Kitchen Table Magick series. Each book in the series addresses a specific area of magick (love, money, psychic development, etc.), and is written in a simple "recipe" format for people who want to use magick in their lives immediately. The Kitchen Table Magick series is akin to a Julia Childs recipe book, only these books contain magickal recipes for people to cook up some miraculous and magickal manifestations in their lives.

Because this series was designed so that each person could pick and choose to read just the books that pertain to their current life situation, each book is meant to be readable as a stand-alone book. To introduce the new reader to the series, this introduction to the series is repeated at the beginning of each book. If you have already read one or more books in this series, please feel free to jump ahead to the recipes that interest you. At the same time, some people feel that reviewing the introduction, as well as the "Rules and

1

Tips," is helpful before diving in. In magickal circles, your will is the guideline so choose whichever route best suits you... the Universe and magickal beings will follow!

## What is Magick?

Many people have multiple different ideas about what magick is or can be. For the sake of clarity, here is what we know about magick after more than 35 years of study and practice. Magick is a precision science! It is also:

- The science of deliberate creation.
- The science of effective prayer.
- The science of manifesting Higher Will (substitute whatever Higher Force is most familiar to you) on the energetic and material planes.
- The science of heightened awareness, selective perception, and dynamic, harmonious relationships.
- The study of intention (as per Aleister Crowley, one of the greatest magickal practitioners in history).
- The system of creation, not coercion. Note: The word manipulation is often used in conjunction with magick, but manipulation simply means the use of the hands. It should be an "OK" word without a lot of charge, but currently it is used mostly to mean coercion. Look it up!
- The principle that every intentional act is a magickal act! Magick gives us the ability to communicate with beings on all levels, and allows us to understand, through direct experience, the actual workings of the Universe.
- The traditional path of spiritual growth.
- Not extraordinary knowledge. It is the "normal" way of life. We've just lost access to it. When you have this kind of knowledge in your understanding, you have the ability to resolve spiritual questions that otherwise become catechism. From a magickal point of view, catechism is not acceptable since a practitioner must experience and verify everything for him or herself. It

avoids the trap of dogma. In past times, having a magickal foundation was essential so that we could talk directly to higher beings in the Universal hierarchy.

- Necessary to effective religious practice.

There is some confusion as to how to spell the word "magick." There are three different commonly used spellings: magick, magic, and majick. Eliphas Levi first used the form "magick" to differentiate religious or ceremonial from stage magick. All forms of spelling are acceptable in what this author teaches.

*"I love Kitchen Table Magick! It's the best mix of both mystical and down-to-earth magick I have ever encountered. The fact that I can use items from my pantry is so handy and fun! It literally is about cooking up magic at my kitchen table, and having love show up in the least expected places!"*
*~ Wendy J., Skokie, IL*

## Is Magick Real?

Yes. Magick is very real and has existed as a precise science for thousands of years. Whether you use the word magick or another name, this spiritual practice is very real. Every single person can learn to do magick. We are ALL born with the talents and abilities that empower us to do magick. The only reason that magick seems so, well, magickal is that this society no longer teaches the art and science of magick. In the distant past, magickal study was just as important as math, science, or the arts. In fact, magick was and still is the birthright of EVERY planetary citizen.

Can you learn to do the kind of magick portrayed in the movies? Yes... and no. The movies are great at giving you a taste of what you can do with magick, but they are not very accurate. In the Harry Potter movies, for instance, the characters use their Wands for every magickal operation. In reality, you can only use the Wand to handle Air energies. Your Wand would actually explode or catch fire if you tried to use it to throw Firebolts and Fireballs as the characters do in the movie.

So, what can you actually do with magick? Quite a lot. Here is a short list to get you started:

- Balance your energies for healing and manifestation
- Change old beliefs
- Defend yourself against physical and psychic attack
- Heal yourself and others
- Find hidden information and see possible futures (and change the future if you do not like the probable futures you divine)
- Psychically communicate with other beings
- Create sacred space
- Find lost people and objects
- Manifest what you want and need in life

At the very basis of magick is the understanding of the four elements: Air, Fire, Water, and Earth. Called elemental magick, these foundational elements are real. Air, Fire, Water, and Earth are part of our natural everyday environment. What makes them magickal is the understanding of how they operate not just on the physical level, but also at the levels of Mind and Spirit.

For instance, while on the physical level, Air is just the stuff we breathe. On the magickal levels Air is the conduit of psychic communication, enlightenment, understanding, dreaming, and more. If you want more of these things in your life, then you need more magickal Air. How do you get more magickal Air? Wear more Air colors, including White for communication and Sky Blue for enlightenment and understanding. To take this one step further, you could also use various magickal techniques to take on more Air to make your body lighter. Take on enough Air and you'll be able to levitate.

By just extending your understanding and use of the

basic ingredients of nature, you are doing magick! Seen in this light, magick isn't all smoke and mirrors, nor is it the result of Hollywood special effects. Magick is the result of truly understanding and working with the very elements that are all around you.

One final note: Many masters, including Wayne Dyer, have said, "You'll see it when you believe it." The same is true for magick. In other words, the suspension of disbelief and the willingness not to exercise contempt prior to investigation are requirements for magick to be "real." Magick is all around us, and always is, but our ability to perceive and use the forces of magick depends on our willingness to be open. No one else can show it to you, only your direct experience and observation can "prove" or demonstrate to you that magick is real.

[this page intentionally left blank]

# *What is Kitchen Table Magick?*

Kitchen Table Magick is exactly what it sounds like—a series of simple recipes that you can literally "cook up" at your kitchen table using household ingredients from your own pantry and cupboard.

The Kitchen Table Magick books have been created for ordinary people who want to mix up a little magick in their lives without all the fancy rituals, but simply with everyday ingredients that can be found in the kitchen pantry, bathroom medicine cabinet, or even stuffed in the back of the junk drawer.

The goal of these books is to allow anyone with the desire to learn this craft to mix up magick literally at the kitchen table using simple recipes. What goes into a simple recipe?

- Everyday items as ingredients
- Easy to follow instructions that don't require years of training
- Procedures that take less than two hours from start to finish
- Built-in expertise that allows the magick to do the heavy lifting
- Some friendly advice on how you can help your magickal recipe provide the best results
- Oh, and a few little rules and guidelines about magickal practice in this specific arena that will keep you safe and sound, magickally speaking, when you use these recipes

## Kitchen Table Magick Equals:
Quick – Effective – Safe – Everyday Use – Ordinary
Affordable Ingredients

## Why Use Kitchen Table Magic?
- Everyone can do magick.
- Magick should be simple, effective, and start working right away, else it is not magick.
- Not everyone has the time or resources to enroll in a school.
- People ask us for magickal help in hundreds of emails everyday... Kitchen Table Magick is designed to help these very people.
- Of the many areas of life, most people only seem to need help in one or two areas, so you need only buy those Kitchen Table Magick books that apply to your needs.
- Magick is for the masses, and should be accessible, affordable, and simple to do. This is what our teacher taught us, and this is the legacy we are paying forward as well.
- While there are many more advanced forms of magick, these books are an introduction to that world so that you can dabble, experiment, try things out, see the result, adjust and amend, and generally have fun... just as you would cooking a meal in your kitchen.
- This book is not for the major foodie, but is perfect for the person who needs magickal help right here, right now!

## Who Should Use These Recipes?
- You and anyone you know who would like a little more magick and a little less ordinary reality in their lives.
- Anyone who needs help RIGHT now and doesn't have time to fly to India or Sedona to sit at the feet of a guru.

- Anyone who does not have access to anything but a computer for help and guidance.
- Anyone who wants to do magick and then forget it (all while quietly watching the magick "do its thing").
- Anyone who wants affordable, down to earth magick they can do with regular ingredients in the comfort of home.

## When to Use Kitchen Table Magic: Anytime...
- You need help.
- You don't want to do all the heavy lifting (leave that to the Angels, Spirit Guides, Animal Totems, and so forth).
- You seem stuck in a rut or corner with no way out.
- You've been struggling with a problem for a long time and need a resolution.
- You don't know what to do but you need to do SOMETHING.
- You'd like to learn how to practice the craft.
- You want to live a more magickal life and stop dealing with ordinary hassles all the time.

## How Do We Know These Recipes Work?
- We teach a slew of these recipes in one-day workshops all over the country, via teleconference, and via videoconference. We also email them to people as part of our school's service work or post them on our blogs and articles library.
- We have used them for over 35 years and still do, every single day – literally tested out at our own kitchen tables for over 35 years (and at thousands of kitchen tables around the world) for a quarter century or more.
- We receive all kinds of stories and testimonials from happy successful students.

# Kitchen Table Undoing Magick at Work...

Read the following example to discover how Undoing Magick works in real life...

### Throw Away Life's Problems

*When life gets tough, it can be tempting to just throw up our hands and give up in despair! Luckily, I learned in magick class that the magickal way to deal with life's issues is to throw away river rocks rather than throwing up my hands!*

*I learned that I could "connect" any problems in my life with inanimate objects, such as rocks. The whole magickal ritual has become a deep and soothing kind of meditation whenever life throws me a curve ball.*

*The ritual is so simple. It goes like this. Whenever I have a problem, I write a list of the different aspects of that problem that I want to toss out of my life. For instance, I was having trouble letting go of a* relationship, even though the breakup occurred months ago. My mind just could not stop circling around the "woulda, coulda, shoulda" mantra. I kept trying to make contact with my former partner, even though we agreed that we would be better off having no contact with each other. I knew I needed to move on, but I just could not seem to do that.

The next step in the ritual is to write a list of aspects of the problem that I wanted to toss out of my life. I wrote down items like:

- circular and repeating thoughts about the relationship,
- anger over certain disagreements between me and my ex,
- regrets over words and actions,
- … and so on (being careful never to attach a rock to a person).

When the list was complete, I grabbed the list and a cloth bag, and then I went to a nearby park that bordered a river. Walking along the river, I chose a rock for each item on my list. I held each rock in my dominant (right) hand and focused intensely the listed item that I wanted to "connect" to the rock. At the same time, I flowed energy down my arm, into my hand, and into the rock. When the rock felt warm or heavy, I knew that the connection had been made. I put the rock into the bag, and continued the process with the next rock as I walked. Even before the process was complete, the walk had become like a meditation, and I felt more peaceful inside.

*When every item on my list had been magickally connected to a rock in my bag, I went to the riverbank. With each rock I took out of my bag, I held the rock while saying the disconnect litany. Then I threw the rock as far as I could into the river. As I emptied my bag, I felt a sense of relief, like a burden had been lifted.*

*After doing the ritual, I still thought about the relationship, but I no longer obsessed about it. I could easily shift my attention to a different topic. As the weeks went by, I stopped thinking about the relationship altogether, except occasionally in passing or in dreams.*

*I liked the effect of this ritual so much that I started using it for all kinds of problems that popped up in my life. It worked equally well for big and small problems. More importantly, I felt like the ritual was super soothing to my soul... the process itself, not only the result. I am most thankful to have learned how to turn an ordinary rock into a problem-solving tool!*

*~ Jake A., Grand Forks, ND*

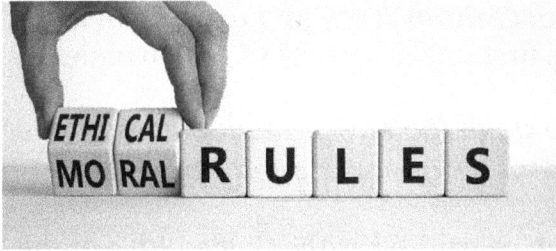

# A Few Rules and Tips About Kitchen Table Magick

As with any game, the game of life has its own set of rules. Specifically, the spiritual side of life has rules. Play by those rules and you will stay safe and easily attract what you want into your life. Break those rules and all types of unwanted consequences happen.

These "spiritual rules" are ones that have been observed, both in personal spiritual practice and spiritual practice with various associated groups and teachers. These rules universally govern any spiritual practice and appear to be in effect whether you know them or not. Unlike ethics and morals, which change with culture and time, these spiritual rules appear to have remained the same throughout time, unchanging, like physical and scientific rules.

The rules in the following section are adapted from *Rules of the Road*, as created by George Dew, co-founder of the Church of Seven Arrows. There are two major rules, which are common to most spiritual practices, along with some minor rules that are specific to our form of magickal practice.

## Two Major Rules

These two rules will probably sound familiar, as they appear in most major religions and spiritual practices, most probably because they are common-sense and apply not just to spiritual practice, but to life as well.

### First Rule: Golden Rule or Law of Karma
This first rule is literally a "golden oldie":

*What you do to the environment or to other beings in the environment brings similar effects back to you in your life.*

Often recognized as the Golden Rule or the Law of Karma, this rule tops the list because it reminds all spiritual practitioners of potential unwanted "rebound" or side effects. As your spiritual power, focus, and abilities grow, this rule will have an ever-greater impact on your life unless you exercise caution. The Universe responds more strongly and powerfully to those with focus, power, and ability.

**Note**: As humanity moves further in the Aquarian Age, many spiritual practitioners have seen more effects from this rule occur faster. In the past, effects of this rule that often took lifetimes to manifest now occur in minutes, days, weeks, or months. In this particular time in Earth's history, karma seems to operate under a "pay as you go" system. Simply stated, expect the effects of the Law of Karma to occur quickly.

### Second Rule: The Judgment of "Good and Bad" According to the Universe
This second rule adds clarity and detail to the first rule described previously:

*If you are unsure whether your acts are "good or bad"-- that is, whether those acts are in keeping with universal laws on this planet—the Universe will reflect its judgment back to you quickly, according to the "pay as you go" Law of Karma.*

This law holds as true for individuals as it does for entire communities, states, nations, or other organized groups. If you are still unsure of the feedback you receive from the Universe, check areas such as your level of health, the soundness of social relationships, your prosperity or lack of, sufficiency of various needs in life, and even your "luck" with appliances and machines. If your luck appears to be consistently poor, then you are probably acting contrary to universal governing laws, regardless of your intentions. The Universe cares about what you do more than what you intend.

### *Additional Detailed Rules*
The following rules offer more detailed standards by which to measure your acts or the acts of others to determine whether these acts are in accordance with universal laws.

- Do nothing that will harm another being unless you are willing to suffer similar or greater harm. What the Universe considers "harm" may be different than what you consider harm.
- Do not bind another being unless you are willing to be similarly bound. An example of binding someone is doing acts in attempt to coerce a specific other person to love you. There is no problem with attracting your soul mate into your life, but doing acts that attempt to coerce a specific other person to love you is a type of binding.
- Never use your spiritual abilities in vain, to show off, or to boost your pride. Using your spiritual abilities from a place of pride usually causes the Universe to bring instant backlash into your life.
- If you choose to charge money or barter for using your spiritual abilities in the service of others, avoid charging extremely high prices. Charge prices for using methods comparable to other professionals, such as an attorney or accountant.
- Never use any spiritual word, chant, litany, or similar "device" unless you are confident in your understanding of its methods, intents, and effects.
- When undertaking a major spiritual operation—one that will require significant effort or attempts to create a major effect in the world—use divination to determine whether you can safely benefit from such

an operation, and to discover the obstacles you must overcome. Divination methods such as pendulum readings, channeling, meditation, and question circles (to name a few) can reveal hidden factors of which you may be unaware.

- In any spiritual endeavor, take your time, think it through, and do it right!

The good news is that you can still do Undoing magick rituals. The ones we teach in this book won't get you in trouble with the Universe while also allowing you to let go of or undo unsavory situations in your life.

# The Ingredients of Undoing Magick

*"Peace comes not from doing, but from undoing; not from getting, but from letting go."*
*-- Swami Satchidananda*

In magick we say that if you understand the Four Magickal Elements, there is nothing you cannot understand in the Universe. Everything in the Universe is made up of some combination of the Four Elements: Air, Water, Fire, and Earth. If you understand this and know how to work with these Four Elements, you can understand and create anything you wish to.

Similarly, you can use the Four Elements and associated tools to undo almost anything in the Universe. Once you understand how something is created, you will also see the way to back track and take that thing apart or undo it. This is one of the reasons for keeping all your magickal procedures written down in a Book of Shadows. If you have performed a reading, a divination, a spell, or some other magickal procedure and are not getting the results you desire, you may need to go back and find the glitch and make corrections or undo the entire thing and start over. In this ebook, we will give you recipes on "undoing" using magickal techniques that can help in ridding yourself of unwanted energies, problems, issues, thoughts, or feelings.

[this page intentionally left blank]

# *Undoing Magick Appetizer Recipes*

## Appetizers: Self Balancing with Undoing Magick

### *Elemental Undoings*

### *Come Back to Present*

*"I have to admit that I am the main person in my life that screws up my life. Unfortunate, right? That's why I love undoing magick. It get a magickal do-over... and trust me, I need as many of those as I can get!"*
*~ Joseph R., Warwick, RI*

[this page intentionally left blank]

# *Elemental Undoings*

*"The unity of four elements is what constitutes and sustains
our existence in this world."*
*~ John O'Donohue*

**Time Required: Fifteen Minutes Per Recipe**

Each of the Four Elements corresponds to different
parts of a person. Air deals with mind and mental processes.
Fire deals with will, desire, and force. Water deals with
emotions. Earth deals with the physical body. Keeping this in
mind can help you choose the best way to get rid of a
problem according to what issue or problem you would like
to rid yourself of. For example, if you are angry and want to
undo your anger, a Fire Element technique works best. If you
are worried about an upcoming event and can't turn off the
negative thoughts, then an Air Element technique would
work better. In this recipe we will give you an undoing
technique for each of the Four Elements so that you can
choose the most appropriate for your issue or problem.

## Air: Dump Boxes of White

An air box is an energetic box filled with an Air Element color (Clear [physical], White [mental], or Sky Blue [spiritual]) created by the aura energy of your hands. These boxes can be used to increase or decrease the amount of a particular type of Air Element energy to balance your overall energy. Too much Air and you may find yourself worried or having obsessive thinking. Too little Air can leave you unfocused, having trouble concentrating, or problems with memory.

## Ingredients

- Color source for Clear, White, or Sky Blue
- Your own two hands
- Square mailing box (optional if you need to practice the hand movements around a physical box shape)

## Recipe Directions

1. Have a Clear, White, or Sky Blue color source available before you start building your box. As you form your box, make the following hand motions in a smooth, unbroken pattern.

2. Form the top and bottom of the box by placing your hands, palms facing each other as if holding a box between them with hands on top and bottom of the box. Start with your hands farther apart and bring them together, "pressing" the energy together.

3. Form the front and back of the box, moving your hands again with palms facing in a position as if you were holding a box on its front and back sides. Press the energy together in this position.

4. Use your hands now in the same way to form the left and right sides of the box.

5. Leave your hands in this last position, as it will hold together as long as you hold the sides of the box.

6. Look at the color source you have selected according to whether you are undoing something physical (Clear), mental (White), or spiritual (Sky Blue) and blow that color out of your body into the box until the box is full. Looking at the color sets your intention on the energy type you are accessing.

7. Destroy the box by throwing it into a corner of the room (upper corners work great) or breaking it over your knee. Be careful not to throw it at a person or animal accidentally since you don't know what consequences could occur with them taking on that particular energy.

## How to Use the Results of Your Recipe

If you want to increase your Air energy, make the box as described, fill it with the appropriate color from your color source by holding the box in front of your eyes and in line with the color source, pulling the color into the box with your intention and "energetic pull" until the box is full. Do not think about this step, just do it. Your intention will do the work. The box is full when your hands grow warm or tingly (about 5-15 seconds). Then bring the box towards your face and "snort" or breathe in the box. If you don't feel any difference within 15 minutes of taking on or taking off a box of Air energy, you can repeat the process and subtract a bit more. The amount you want to rid yourself of can vary according to how much extra you began with.

## Fire: Hug Your Fridge

An excess of Fire Element energy can manifest as pain, stress, anger, inflammation, fever, headache, or anxiety. You can safely ground out your excess Fire energy using large appliances such as a refrigerator or stove, electrical outlets, or light switch plates.

## Ingredients

- Refrigerator or another large grounded electrical appliance
- Sun Yellow candle
- Wooden or paper matches

## Recipe Directions

1. If possible, place the area of pain, stress, or inflammation directly on the refrigerator. For instance, if you have a headache in the front of your head, put your forehead on the refrigerator. If you have a headache in back of your head, put the back of your head on the refrigerator. For general pain or stress all over the body, put your hands on the refrigerator or lie down and put your feet on the refrigerator.

2. Flow all the energy that you don't want, such as pain or anxiety, into the refrigerator. Fire energy flows quickly, so you won't need to flow for more than a minute or two. You don't need to think about how to do this, your body already knows how. Just push the pain out of your body and into the refrigerator.

3. After flowing out all the excess Fire energy, light a Sun Yellow candle (use a bright yellow candle with no orange tones). Cup your hands above and around the candle flame (not too close to avoid getting burned) and pull in healing Yellow energy to replace the energy you've flowed into the refrigerator. This shouldn't take more than a minute or two.

## How to Use the Results of Your Recipe

Do not ground Fire energy out into computers, small electrical appliances, lamps, or electronics as they cannot handle that amount of Fire energy like the large appliances can.

# Water: Feed Your Emotions to a Plant

This recipe uses the same energetic box technique as given above for the Air Element. Water corresponds to emotions and "gut feelings" of happiness, depression, sadness, grief, compassion, and empathy. (Note that passion is Fire as is the emotion of anger, anxiety, and other forceful more radiative type feelings, but compassion and less forceful emotions are Water).

On a physical level, Water energy deals with the circulatory system and glandular system. The Water Element colors are Water Blue for the physical or mundane levels (blue much the color in crayon box marked "blue"), Deep Blue for mental or emotional levels (closer to a dark navy blue color), and Blue Black for spiritual level.

## Ingredients

- Color source for Water Blue or Deep Blue (can be squares of colored paper)
- Your own two hands
- Square mailing box (optional if you need to practice the hand movements around a physical box shape)

## Recipe Directions

1. Have a Water Blue or Deep Blue color source available before you start building your box. We do not recommend using Blue Black unless you are a very experienced practitioner as it can bring up buried unconscious emotions that you may not be able to safely deal with.

2. Create an energy box using the procedure given for making Air Element boxes.

3. Looking at the appropriate color source, flow Water energy down through the tissues in your arms and into the box until it is full.

4. You can then throw the Water box into the Earth, pipes, or even better throw it on a plant or tree as they really appreciate receiving your psychic Water.

## How to Use the Results of Your Recipe

When getting rid of Water boxes, be sure you NEVER throw them into an electrical system like you do with Fire boxes.

If you want to take on more Water energy, be sure you DO NOT breathe in the box like we did above with the Air boxes. Instead, you will pull it up through the tissues in your arms into your body (reverse how you filled the box).

## Earth: Rooting

Rooting is a good way to balance your own Earth energies. You can draw in energies from Mother Earth directly with this technique or flow out Earth energies (or other unwanted energies such as Fire energies) to rid yourself of them. Always be sure to pull your roots back in when you are done – if you stand up without doing so you may feel a slight "popping" sensation and your body will be sore for a few days. Rooting can help you feel refreshed, awake, alive and balanced. You can use this recipe when you are alone or in public and no one will know what you are doing.

## Ingredients

- Comfortable place to sit on a chair or on the floor
- Several minutes of quiet time and space

## Recipe Directions

1. Place your heels, palms, or seat (or all three) on the ground. You can extend roots from more than one body part at once.

2. Envision yourself forming roots from your palms, heels or the base of your spine and begin extending those roots with your intention. You don't need to

think about it, just do it! Some people find it easier to do with eyes closed.

3. Push your roots through the carpet or tile, into the sub floor and down into the Earth. If you are in a multi-level building, you will need to go through each level until you reach the Earth. If you are wearing shoes with thick soles, you may have to extend the roots out the sides of your shoes.

4. Once your roots reach the Earth keep extending them down through the topsoil and deeper layers until you reach bedrock.

5. When you reach bedrock, lock your roots in.

6. Sit quietly with your roots in the Earth and just breathe naturally.

7. With each exhaling breath send any unwanted energies down your roots into the bedrock. You can see these as the colors represented by them or just the feeling and/or pain that you feel. The Earth is highly receptive and will receive these energies easily.

8. With each inhaling breathe pull in minerals, fluids, and other energies from the Earth for nourishment and balancing. You don't have to specify what you're pulling up – your body and your roots will work automatically with the Earth to pull up what is needed.

9. Once you feel relaxed and nourished pull your roots back up into your body. See them drawing back up through all the layers and flooring they went through in being extended. Stay seated until you totally pull your "roots" back in.

## How to Use the Results of Your Recipe

In a loud, noisy crowd, or even an angry crowd, if you can't access an electrical ground to put out the excess Fire energies, you can put down roots and ground the excess Fire energy through your roots. If someone is harassing you physically, mentally, or spiritually, you can put down roots to make yourself more stable and grounded. Push your heels down as you root to push the roots down strongly and quickly. To dump Earth energies quickly, put down roots and push brown with a little water down your roots. It's faster than other forms of direct flowing energy.

# Come Back to Present

*"Do not dwell in the past, do not dream of the future,
concentrate the mind on the present moment."*
*~ Buddha*

**Time Required: Five Minutes**

Dwelling on either the past or the future can keep us trapped in negative emotions such as worry or fear. Freedom from them can occur only in the present. Anytime we are fearful, worried, or stressed, we are either in the past or the future. It is also a magickal principle that all negativity exists in the past or future, not in the present.

Use this recipe anytime you feel things are spinning out of your control, or that you feel "crazy" or chaotic. This recipe gives you a way to call yourself out of the past or future and be grounded in present time, allowing you to regain control of your life again and undo those negative emotional states.

## Ingredients
- A mirror
- Brief time and space to yourself in which you can talk out loud

## Recipe Directions
1. Look at yourself in the mirror. Be sure to look into your own eyes.

2. In a voice of command, say out loud while continuing to look yourself in the eye, *"Come to present time!"*

3. You may have to repeat this several times to make sure you are completely back to present time in your mind and spirit. This command actually speaks to your mind and spirit. Your body always exists in present time, but the command in this ritual tells your mind and spirit to come back to present time as well.

4. Once you are in present time, you no longer will feel chaotic, out of control or "crazy". It's a magickal principle. It's a fact. When you lose the feeling of chaos, being out of control, or any other negative feelings, then you will know your mind and spirit are back in the present.

## How to Use the Results of Your Recipe
If you absolutely are unable to follow this recipe because you don't have access to a mirror or can't speak out loud, you can also free yourself of negative thoughts of the past and future and come back to present time by feeling sensation in your body. You can only have sensation in present time. For example, you can wear a rubber band around your wrist and snap it. The feeling of the rubber band hitting your wrist will bring you back to present time.

# Undoing Magick Main Course Recipes

## Main Courses: Spells for Rewinding and Letting Go

### Pendulum Unwind

### Simple Sendback

### Wash Away Your Cares

*"I used to never understand why my magick teacher taught us that the more powerful we become as magickal practitioners, the more we might attract adverse situations. I still don't know why this is true, but I can say that it is true. I have used protection and undoing magick to shield myself as I attract more adverse situations along my magickal journey. It has really helped me in many situations."*
*~ Barb C., Erie, PA*

[this page intentionally left blank]

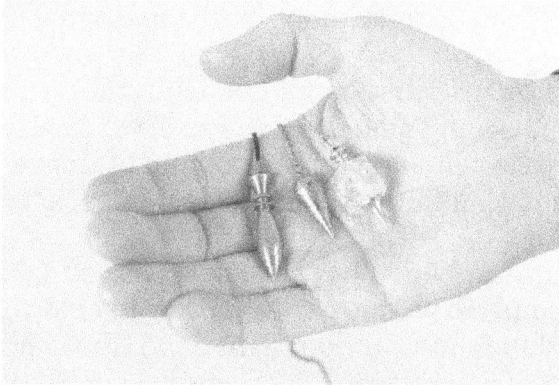

# *Pendulum Unwind*

*"We're waiting for the pendulum to swing back again,*
*which I am absolutely confident it will."*
*~ Don Bluth*

**Time Required: Forty-Five Minutes**

You can use a magickal pendulum to unwind problems or undo situations. Use as many times a day as necessary or as many days in a row as needed for stubborn problems.

## Ingredients
- Paper clip or small stone
- String
- OR pendulum you have purchased

## Recipe Directions
1. Purchase a pendulum or make a pendulum by tying a

paper clip or small stone on the end of a string.

2. First cleanse your pendulum with smoke. The smoke from burning pine resin and sage works well. Just hold the pendulum over a column of smoke from your Firebowl until the smoke begins to "stick" to it.

3. Next, your pendulum needs to be keyed so that it responds to your energies. To key it, hold your pendulum in your dominant hand (the hand you naturally point with). Flow energy into the pendulum for a minute or two, or until it grows warm and tingly.

4. Begin training your pendulum by establishing its yes and no directions. Decide if you want your pendulum to indicate "yes" with a vertical or horizontal swing. The "no" indicator will be the opposite of the "yes" indicator (if "yes" is a vertical swing, then "no" is a horizontal swing). Hold your pendulum suspended from your dominant hand. Rest your elbow on a table or your knee to stabilize your hand and swing your pendulum in a gentle clockwise circle telling it, "Show me yes." Wait for the pendulum to settle into the proper swing (whatever direction you chose). If it doesn't, ask again. Once your pendulum consistently swings in the proper direction for "yes," use the same process to ask it to show you the proper swing for "no."

5. Now you are ready to start training your pendulum to give you actual answers by practicing asking questions about short futures. Ask yes/no questions that can be verified in a 15 - 30 minute time frame. For instance, at the end of the workday you might ask your pendulum, "Will my roommate be home in the next 20 minutes?" Verify the correctness of your pendulum's answer, and then ask another question. In the beginning, it doesn't matter whether your

pendulum gives you the correct answer or not, this is just the practice period and giving your pendulum a lot of practice is the important thing right now. The more you work with your pendulum, the more accurate it will become. Don't get obsessed with the "rightness" of the answers during this training period and avoid getting frustrated and putting those type of negative energies into the process. You don't expect to sit down at a piano the first time and play a beautiful song. This too takes practice.

6. Once you are getting reliable results from the training phase using your pendulum, you can use it to help clear or undo problems or issues that you are struggling with in your life. Start by holding your pendulum in your dominant hand, letting it dangle while you visualize the problem you want to clear.

7. Ask your pendulum, "Can I, May I, Should I, clear this situation?" If you get a yes answer from your pendulum, then move forward. This is an important step because sometimes there is a life lesson to be learned from a specific problem you are facing that should not be interfered with. If the answer is no, stop this procedure.

8. If you have determined it is okay to clear the problem, begin swinging your pendulum in a counterclockwise direction, asking it to clear the situation. As you do this, "see" the situation resolving in your mind. Be very specific with your request and what you envision as to the situation being resolved – not how but what it would look like to not have the problem. The how is the Universe's part.

9. Continue to focus on clearing the situation until your pendulum stops spinning in the counterclockwise direction. It will then either start moving along a

vertical or horizontal axis, stop or start spinning clockwise. When it stops swinging on its own then the problem has been cleared.

## How to Use the Results of Your Recipe

Once a problem has been cleared you can always choose to bring it back if you really want to. But try trusting the power of your pendulum and your intent, and release the problem from your consciousness. If you find it creeping back into your consciousness throughout the day, change your focus to something else. This is a good procedure to use on clearing out repetitive thoughts that you find yourself having, especially in the case of negative thoughts which you want to clear out to avoid attracting those negative situations to you. Instead of visualizing a situation, you want resolved just hold the repetitive thought in your mind and ask your pendulum to clear the thought from your life. After this process, you may still find the thought popping up in your mind occasionally, but it should appear far less frequently than before and eventually will disappear.

# *Simple Sendback*

*"I believe that we live in a "return to sender universe" –
what you send out is exactly what you will get back."
~ Rachele Brooke Smith*

**Time Required: Forty-Five Minutes**

This recipe is a simpler form of a spell sendback. A spell sendback uses Tarot cards to represent a spell that you have found someone else has put on you and sends the energy from that spell back to the originator, thus breaking it. The simple sendback in this recipe does not use the Tarot and although the procedure is similar, it is designed to undo situations and problems sending the energy from them off into the half worlds and releasing it.

## Ingredients
- Two white taper or pillar candles
- A 3"X5" or 4"X6" double-sided camping mirror (make

sure one side is not magnifying)
- A pair of pliers
- A strong rubber band
- Your Book of Shadows
- Your Athame (Fire element tool)
- Your Plate or Pantacle (Earth element tool)
- Index cards
- Sun Yellow candle
- Paper or wooden matches
- Pen or pencil
- Sturdy table or flat surface to lay out sendback

## Recipe Directions

1. Sit in the South facing North.

2. Use the white candles for Wisdom and Protection. Place the candles to the left and to the right of the space where you will set your index cards. The one to your left is the Protection candle and the one to your right is the Wisdom candle.

3. Have your Sun Yellow candle also on the table and charge it by lighting it with your paper or wooden matches, cupping your hands above and around the flame and saying out loud in a strong voice:

*"Child of Wonder,*
*Child of Flame,*
*Nourish My Spirit,*
*and Protect My Aim."*

4. Write the problem or issue you want to undo in your life on an index card. Write your name on another index card or put a picture of yourself instead of using a card.

5. Place the card with your name or the picture of yourself just to the right of the Protection candle (one

to your left). Place the card you have written your problem or issue on just to the left of the Wisdom candle (one to your right).

6. Put your Sun candle on your Plate.

7. Light a match from your Sun candle and light first the Wisdom candle (on your right), then your Protection candle (on your left), then go back across to your Wisdom candle to close the loop. Do all three of these steps with one lit match in a continuous motion.

8. Load your Athame with Electric Blue energy (you can use the blue in your candle flame as the source to pull that energy into your Athame). Perform the same three actions from Step 7 using your Athame with Electric Blue energy, making a loop with a match from Wisdom candle to Protection candle, back to Wisdom candle. This connects the two sides of the sendback space.

9. Clamp the double-sided camping mirror in the pliers so that the mirror rests vertically on its long side flush with the table. Position the pliers so that they just grip the edge of the mirror, enough to hold the mirror securely in a vertical position. Wrap the rubber band around the handles of the pliers to hold them in position.

10. Holding the pliers so that the camping mirror is poised vertically above the center of the index cards (higher than the tops of the candle flames) with one mirrored side facing each candle, deliberately "slice" the sendback space in half by bringing the mirror down into the space and setting it halfway between the two white candles with the cards next to them. Make sure there are no cracks between the edge of the mirror and the table, and that the mirror is in line

with the cards and candles.

11. Slowly and carefully slide your Plate with the Sun Yellow candle on it to the right of the card with your name or your picture and to the left of the mirror. Make sure you don't put your head into the space. The Sun candle helps you overcome the negative effects of your problem or issue that you are undoing.

12. Now load your Athame again with Electric Blue energy and use it to draw two loops in Electric Blue. The first loop is drawn from the Wisdom candle down to the top edge of the mirror and back to the Wisdom candle. The second loop is drawn from the Protection candle down to the top edge of the mirror and back to the Protection candle.

13. Observing fire safety rules, let the candles burn for 30 minutes and then blow them out.

14. During that time, record exactly the steps you took and all the information in your Book of Shadows. This is an important step in case you need to back track or make any adjustments in the future. Write the time you started, the date, the time you stopped, what the problem or issue was, whether you used a picture or card with your name on it and anything else that will give you the most complete record of the procedure.

## How to Use the Results of Your Recipe

Remember, as we've stated in other recipes, when you start practicing to develop your undoing, don't get frustrated with initial results. Learning to ignore the outcome is one of the keys to success. Over time your undoing will get stronger and more accurate. In the beginning, don't worry about if your results are "right" or not.

# *Wash Away Your Cares*

*"The secret to success is to be in harmony with existence, to always be calm to let each wave of life wash us a little farther up the shore."*
*~ Cyril Connolly*

**Time Required: Fifteen Minutes**

Rain and moving water can be a magickal tool to help you undo situations, old patterns and habits, and other negative things inside yourself. The element of Water has long been used since tribal times for cleansing and to help in releasing the old and bringing in the new. By walking in the rain or running water, old beliefs that no longer serve are washed away by the running water while new ideas, insights, and inspiration come from the rain above.

## Ingredients
- A place you can walk by a source of running water

such as a river or stream, fountain, or spillway
- A rainy day

## Recipe Directions

1. If you can, find a place in nature where you can walk in the rain by running water (for this version, you would have to perform this ritual on a rainy day). Make sure you are walking by running water such as a river, a stream, a fountain, or spillway, and not standing water as standing water is stagnant. Stagnant water does not do a great job of carrying negativity away from you.

2. As you walk by or stand in the running water, feel your old beliefs and worries fall away, being carried by the flow of the water to be recycled in some other form, in some other place in the Universe. Also release any repetitive thoughts, feelings of anxiety, and anything negative you want to release.

3. As you stand under the rain, feel the brightness and refreshment of the new bursting into your world-- new ideas, new will to work, new expressions of creativity, and new feelings of all kinds.

4. If you want, you can also pray to whatever powers and beings inspire you, telling them exactly what you want to release and envision that energy flowing away in the moving water. Also tell them what you'd like to welcome into your life and envision it coming down to you in the rain.

## How to Use the Results of Your Recipe

If you find yourself needing this ritual at a time when it is raining and can get to a source of running water such as a river or stream, then great; you're all set. However, you might find this situation of rain and getting out into nature by running water does not fit into your schedule or you need the ritual on a sunny day. Instead, you can turn to your shower. This is an easy alternative to get fresh water from above and running water below, and chances are you already shower daily. Just follow the same directions as in the above steps using the shower for running water below and falling water from above.

[this page intentionally left blank]

# Undoing Magick Dessert Recipes

## Desserts: Get More Information or Get Rid of the Unwanted

### Grounding Stone

### Coffee Cup Scrying

*"I sometimes find myself wandering around in circles in life. That's when I turn to the Universe—either to helps me get more information so I can get centered, or to dump unwanted factors in my life. The coffee cup scrying technique is one of my favorites because I am literally practicing magick in plain sight... and it works!"*
*~ Gemma I., Newark, DE*

[this page intentionally left blank]

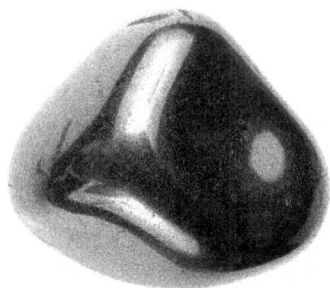

# Grounding Stone

*"When someone is properly grounded in life, they shouldn't
have to look outside themselves for approval."*
*~ Epictetus*

**Time Required: Twenty Minutes**

This recipe gives you a way to connect with Earth
energy to ground out that which you wish to undo in your
life. Hematite is a grounding stone that easily "pulls" and
attracts energy, making it the perfect magickal tool for
grounding out unwanted energy. This simple magick recipe
gives you a way to dump the negative energy associated with
your problem, issue, or situation into a hematite stone.

## Ingredients
- A sample of hematite
- (Optional) paper and pencil or pen to write Directors,
  Limiters, and verses
- Material made of natural fiber or a small bag made of

natural fiber

## Recipe Directions

1. Hold the hematite stone in your dominant hand (the hand with which you naturally point).

2. Focus on the problem or issue that you want to undo in your life and flow those unwanted energies into the hematite stone. This is not a thinking exercise. Just will it, feel yourself pushing that energy out into the stone, and it will happen.

3. When the stone feels tingly or warm, you have grounded the unwanted energies into the stone.

4. Wrap the stone in a natural material, like cotton or wool, or place in a small bag made of natural material to store it safely.

5. Put it away in a safe place where no one will find it and open it or bury it in the ground deep enough that it will not be found.

## How to Use the Results of Your Recipe

This procedure sends the problem into the half worlds. You may also want to write Directors, Limiters, and possibly even verses if you are dealing with a complicated or multi-faceted problem or issue. Doing this will turn the procedure into more of a spell matrix and add force and power to it. Simply write on a piece of paper the Directors (exactly what you want to accomplish or what you are asking for) and the Limiters (what you do not want to have happen as a result of the spell) and read them aloud while you are flowing the energy into the hematite stone. If you also write spell verses, you would read them out loud at this time also.

Here is an example of turning this into a spell matrix:

- **Problem**: Wish to remove my negative thoughts

48

about not being able to find a good job.

- **Directors**: I want to secure a job within the next 3 months that pays a minimum of $60,000.00 a year, in my field of study with sociology, is within a 20 mile radius of my family and my friend Bill, and will allow me to work with others I respect and treat me with respect.
- **Limiters**: I want the job to require me only to do tasks that are legal or that I would consider ethical, and I would not get the job as the result of death or harm to anyone else or harm to property.
- Then you might use these Directors and Limiters write a **verse such as**: "Within 3 months a job I need, sixty thousand dollars a year would hold me in good stead, close to home so getting to work is snappy, working in sociology would totally make me happy. etc...." (keep going adding in the limiters)

[this page intentionally left blank]

# Coffee Cup Scrying

*"It's amazing how the world begins to change through the eyes of a cup of coffee."*
*~ Donna A. Favors*

**Time Required: Forty-Five Minutes**

Change the problem you want to undo on a spirit level by talking to spirit beings involved through a cold cup of coffee acting as a scrying tool. Cold coffee gives you a flat dark surface to scry as a way of divination or communicating with spirit beings that can provide guidance on how to undo your problem or who can remove your problem from you in some cases.

## Ingredients
- Coffee (instant or filtered)
- Cup or mug
- Flat surface such as a table or counter to set cup on

51

- Comfortable place to sit to be able to see into the cup
- Knowledge of directions South and North or a compass to find them
- At least 30 minutes of quiet, uninterrupted time and space
- Pen or pencil
- Paper, notebook, or Book of Shadows

## Recipe Directions

1. Make some coffee (any kind will do -- filtered or instant) or buy a cup of already made coffee (plain black). Wait for the coffee to cool down to room temperature.

2. Put the coffee in any cup or mug that has a large enough surface for you to see into it.

3. Once your cup of coffee has cooled sit in the South facing North with the cup of coffee in front of you on a flat surface such as table or counter.

4. Be sure you will not be disturbed for at least 30 minutes since scrying requires concentration and a quiet space.

5. Once you are comfortably settled, gently place both hands around the cup of coffee and flow some energy from your dominant hand (hand you naturally point with) through the cup of coffee into your non-dominant hand. Continue to flow that energy up the arm and shoulder of your non-dominant hand, then across your back, then down the arm of your dominant hand.

6. Keep flowing energies in this circle for a minute or so until the coffee cup feels charged or energized. You are now ready to scry.

7. Scrying is simply asking the Universe to provide you with the information you seek and using a visual surface to view the communications being sent. Since you are asking for information that pertains to you personally, there is no need to worry that you are invading anyone else's privacy. You may wish to also invite angels, spiritual guides, or other higher beings that have any knowledge and help to offer pertaining to your particular problem or issue.

8. Be sure to thank all beings or the Universe for the help they are about to provide before you begin scrying.

9. Now calmly and quietly look into the surface of the coffee. Gently unfocus your eyes while still looking into the surface of the coffee.

10. Next become very curious about the problem or issue you wish to undo in your life. Allow questions about it to float softly through your mind as you continue to look into the coffee cup. Ask questions such as "What is causing this problem?", "What could help me get over or around this problem?", "What am I not seeing that is preventing me from moving forward or getting past this problem?", "Is there a reason I should not release this problem and a lesson I need to learn from it?", etc...

11. Use whatever questions come to you naturally that pertain to your particular situation. Keep asking these questions softly in your mind, allowing your eyes to remain unfocused and allowing answers to drift into your consciousness.

12. Be prepared for answers to arrive in all shapes and sizes. Sometimes you will see images from your past. Other times you will experience feelings and sensations that call up memories. You may also

receive short phrases, images, ideas, physical jolts, or long strings of information. Do not worry about writing these down right now. You don't need to interrupt the flow as this information will remain in your consciousness long after you stop scrying.

13. Once you have enough information--or the flow of information stops—once again thank the spirit beings, guides, angels, or the Universe for the information that you have received.

14. Now take the time to write down all the information you received in your notebook or Book of Shadows. Don't worry if the information doesn't all make sense right now. You will find that the pieces of information you received will form a cohesive picture in the days to come.

15. If the bits of information are not clear to you, simply read the notes you jotted down each day and ask a higher being to help you clarify the information you received (always thanking them in advance for the help you are about to receive). Keep asking for help and guidance. Within seven days you should have clarity about the root of your problem.

## How to Use the Results of Your Recipe

This recipe gives you a way to obtain information on the root of the problem and guidance on how to remove it or if you should or shouldn't remove it. If there is a spiritual lesson that requires you go through the difficulty, then it may be that you need to leave it alone. If the information you received makes sense to you and is alright to remove, you may use the recipe for Pendulum Unwind included in this ebook or you may ask a particular spirit being or the Universe to remove the problem or issue from you. This will depend more specifically on what the problem or issue is that you are undoing.

# *More Magickal Resources*

## Kindle or Paperback on Amazon:
1. ***Witchcraft Spell Book Series:***
   - Learn How to Do Witchcraft Rituals and Spells with Your Bare Hands (Witchcraft Spell Books, Book 1)
   - Learn How to Do Witchcraft Rituals and Spells with Household Ingredients (Witchcraft Spell Books, Book 2)
   - Learn How to Do Witchcraft Rituals and Spells with Magical Tools (Witchcraft Spell Books, Book 3)
   - Witchcraft Spell Book: The Complete Guide of Witchcraft Rituals & Spells for Beginners (compilation of Books 1, 2, & 3)
2. ***Kitchen Table Magick Series***

## Ebooks and Online Courses at *www.shamanschool.com*
   - Wand: Air Tool
   - Athame: Fire Tool
   - Chalice: Water Tool
   - Plate: Earth Tool
   - Magical Tool: Firebowl
   - Psychic Development
   - Energy Healing For Self and Others

- How to Do Voodoo
- Daily Rituals to Attract What You Want in Life

***Find a complete list of magickal resources on https://amzn.to/3swxvPo. These resources are constantly updated so check back often!***

# Free Gift Offer

To thank you for purchasing this book, I'd like to give you a

100% FREE GIFT

Learn more about your free magickal gift.

## Access Your Free Gift at
## www.shamanschool.com

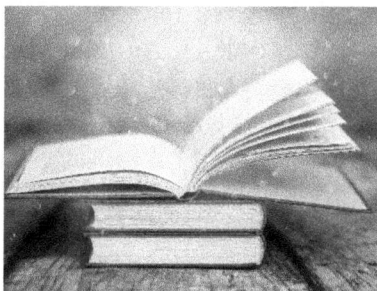

*Find a complete list of magickal resources on https://amzn.to/3swxvPo. These resources are constantly updated so check back often!*

# About G. Alan Joel

Magick means many things to different people. The form of magick taught by G. Alan Joel for more than 30 years is steeped in tribal traditions from around the world, from both modern tribal cultures and those from the past, which have been mostly passed on through oral dialog.

At the very heart of the magick that Mr. Joel teaches is the use of Universal Laws for the benefit of self, others, and even the planet. These magickal traditions can take on many forms, including simple rituals for daily use, specific spells for particular life situations, the use of simulacra (often better known as voodoo), weather working, water witching, the use of the elemental tools (Firebowl, Wand, Athame, Chalice, and Plate), magickal self-defense rituals, and more. Also included are the use of the Tarot for divination and spellwork, divination rituals of all kinds, Spirit-to-Spirit communication, exercises for psychic development, and abundant healing techniques.

Through his 30 plus years of studying, teaching, and honing his magickal practice, G. Alan Joel has helped thousands of people successfully integrate the magickal, and seemingly miraculous, into their daily lives. In fact, one of the greatest gifts Mr. Joel has offered through his teachings is the ability for his students to always find a magickal solution for life situations that often seem impossible to solve. With magick, anything is possible in the mundane world. All that is required of the practitioner is an open mind, the desire to learn, and a willingness to pay some time and effort into his or her magickal practice. One of Mr. Joel's favorite quotes is:

*"What you pay into your practice pays you back!"*

While many magickal traditions have fiercely guarded their secrets from the public, Mr. Joel feels that "Magick is the birthright of every planetary citizen." As such he strives to offer magickal teachings that are easily learned and inexpensive (no excessive fees to join exclusive magickal groups or ascend up the levels of learning). He also offers techniques that are usable and effective for all who are sincere in their desire to practice magick. In essence, Mr. Joel's methods teach a form of "Every Man's (and Woman's) Magick." All are welcome, his teachings are simple yet effective, and he also offers online classes in which he helps students troubleshoot their magickal issues in an interactive setting.

Find out more about Mr. Joel's teachings here and on his website (***www.shamanschool.com***) where magickal offerings are updated on a regular basis.

Mr. Joel augments this magickal knowledge and teaching with 30 years of practice as Doctor of Chinese Medicine, including a deep understanding of herbology and acupuncture. His understanding of the healing arts deepens the magickal knowledge he teaches, as magickal healing is a major aspect of his teachings. Mr. Joel believes that while there is clearly a time and place for Western Medicine, magickal and Eastern healing techniques can be harmoniously blended in to offer people many choices for healing all types of health conditions.

# About the Esoteric School of Shamanism and Magic

The Esoteric School of Shamanism and Magic was started from a desire for all people from all over the globe to be able to attend a real, if virtual, school dedicated to magick and shamanism. The aim of the Esoteric School of Shamanism and Magic is to help people create permanent, positive change in their lives through the study of esoteric magickal and shamanic knowledge. It doesn't matter what your esoteric background is, whether you started out with witchcraft, religious studies, spirituality or candle magick, we welcome you. We believe that the Truth is the same, no matter which form you practice. We delight in all manner of shamanic schools and traditions, magickal techniques and esoteric ritual. You can visit us at ***www.shamanschool.com***, our blog at ***http://shamanmagic.blogspot.com***, or on social media via links on our website.

[this page intentionally left blank]

[this page intentionally left blank]

[this page intentionally left blank]

[this page intentionally left blank]

www.ingramcontent.com/pod-product-compliance
Lightning Source LLC
Chambersburg PA
CBHW071929020426
42331CB00010B/2790